Read & Respond

FOR
KS2

SECTION
1

James and the Giant Peach
Teachers' notes 3

SECTION
2

Guided reading
Teachers' notes 4

SECTION
3

Shared reading
Teachers' notes 7
Photocopiable extracts 8

SECTION
4

Plot, character and setting
Activity notes 11
Photocopiable activities 15

SECTION
5

Talk about it
Activity notes 19
Photocopiable activities 22

SECTION
6

Get writing
Activity notes 25
Photocopiable activities 28

SECTION
7

Assessment
Teachers' notes and activity 31
Photocopiable activity 32

Read & Respond

FOR KS2

Author: Huw Thomas

Editor: Victoria Lee

Assistant Editor: Rachel Mackinnon

Series Designer: Anna Oliwa

Designer: Helen Taylor

Illustrations: Quentin Blake

Text © 2006 Huw Thomas © 2006 Scholastic Ltd

Designed using Adobe InDesign
Published by Scholastic Ltd, Villiers House,
Clarendon Avenue, Leamington Spa,
Warwickshire CV32 5PR
www.scholastic.co.uk

Printed by Bell & Bain

2 3 4 5 6 7 8 9   8 9 0 1 2 3 4 5

British Library Cataloguing-in-Publication Data
A catalogue record for this book is available from the British
Library.

ISBN 0-439-94492-9   ISBN 978-0439-94492-2

The right of Huw Thomas to be identified as the author of this
work has been asserted by him in accordance with the Copyright,
Designs and Patents Act 1988.

Extracts from The National Literacy Strategy © Crown
copyright. Reproduced under the terms of HMSO Guidance
Note 8.

Acknowledgements

The publishers gratefully acknowledge permission to reproduce the
following copyright material:
David Higham Associates for the use of text extracts from *James
and the Giant Peach* by Roald Dahl © 1961, Roald Dahl Nominee
Ltd (1961, Penguin; 1973, Penguin). **Penguin Books Limited** for
the use of illustrations and front cover in its entirety from *James
and the Giant Peach* by Roald Dahl and illustrated by Quentin
Blake. Text © 1961, Roald Dahl Nominee Limited, illustration
© 1995, Quentin Blake (1961, Penguin; 1973, Puffin).
Every effort has been made to trace copyright holders for the works
reproduced in this book, and the publishers apologise for any
inadvertent omissions.

James and the Giant Peach

About the book

James and the Giant Peach is a fantasy adventure story in which a child living with his cruel aunts is transported away from miserable circumstances.

Having a happy young childhood, James's parents are tragically eaten by a rhinoceros while visiting London. James is sent to live with his aunts, who treat him cruelly and do not let him leave their house on the hill. One day a strange man brings magic to the house and a giant peach grows in the garden.

One night, while James is cleaning up from the people who visited the peach in the day, he finds a hole leading inside the peach. Inside he encounters fantastic, overgrown creatures, with whom he escapes, in the peach, to the USA. Their Atlantic journey involves dangerous encounters with cliffs, sharks, Cloud-Men and an aeroplane.

The book includes a succession of memorable characters, from the two wicked aunts to the Centipede, the 'pest' on the peach.

About the author

Born in Wales in 1916, of Norwegian parents' Roald Dahl is one of the best-known writers of children's fiction.

As a child he attended boarding schools where he experienced discipline which he always looked back on as cruel and barbarous, but in the middle of this horror he always recalled 'blessed, beautiful Mrs O'Connor', a woman who would come and read to the boys at his school on a Saturday afternoon. It was here that he developed a love of literature.

He began writing after being injured in a terrible plane crash. The *Hornblower* author, CS Forester, suggested he write about his adventures and the resulting short story, 'A Piece of Cake', proved to be a success.

Roald Dahl wrote two books of autobiography, *Boy* and *Going Solo*. The former contains a fantastic story about a dead mouse in a sweet shop – well worth a read.

In writing about being an author, Dahl gave two important snippets of advice. The first was: 'You should have a lively imagination', something he exhibited with his giant peaches, friendly giants, flying glass elevators and cunning poachers. He also advised: 'You must have strong self-discipline', explaining that the writer often works alone, so must keep themselves at work. Roald Dahl himself worked in a shed at the end of his garden.

Dahl's works have their critics. His portrayals of some characters have been seen as cruel and stereotypical. He also expressed some controversial political views in his non-fiction writing for adults. However, his children's books include some of the most successful titles written for children, including *Charlie and the Chocolate Factory* and *The BFG*. He once wrote: 'A good plot is like a dream', adding that, when it is thought up, such a plot should be quickly written down, or else it may be forgotten.

Roald Dahl died in 1990 at the age of 74.

Facts and figures
James and the Giant Peach
First published in the USA in 1961 by Alfred A Knopf Inc and in the UK in 1967 by Allen & Unwin.
Roald Dahl
Won the Whitbread Award for *The Witches* in 1983. In 1988 he won the Children's Book Award for *Matilda*. Roald Dahl wrote many of his books in a small hut at the bottom of his garden.

Guided reading

Introducing the book

Begin by asking the children about the name Roald Dahl. Some of them may have encountered other books by the author, or films based on his work – there tends to be a film made every five years of one of his stories. As they list the titles they know, ask the children to tell you what they can remember from these tales. Make a note of any common features that emerge between stories: children in miserable circumstances, horrible villains, and the place of magic in his tales.

It is at this point you need to tackle the fact that some of the class may already be familiar with *James and the Giant Peach*. Explain that, if they have seen the film, they can relive it through the book. If children have listened to the story on tape or read it at home, say that reading it in a group will help them to explore the story further, but ask them to do their best not to provide 'plot-spoilers' at every reading.

Turn their attention to the blurb on the back of the book. Just from reading this, what can they see that reminds them of other Roald Dahl tales?

Chapters 1 to 5

Read the opening of Chapter 1 to the children and then ask them to read on as far as the end of Chapter 2. By this stage, the misery of life with the two aunts has been established.

Read together the opening two paragraphs of Chapter 3. Who could this man be? Is he bound to be good for James? (Think of 'Rumpelstiltskin'.) Ask the children to read to the end of Chapter 3. Clearly there is magic at work here. Whether or not they know the story, ask the children to think of as many different things that *could* happen as a result of James using the magic things. Note that, at this stage, the magic things are the main ingredients of a potion, and nothing to do with peaches and soil. Should James drink it? Would they?

Ask the children to read to the end of Chapter 5. How do they feel as James's hope of rescue slithers down into the soil? One of the problems of reading a well-known story, popularised through film, is that the children know what happens next. Ask them to imagine the event as a first time reader. What would they think of these events?

Chapters 6 to 14

Read Chapters 6 and 7 together and ask the children: 'What is going on?'. At this stage the connection between the magic things and the peach growing is not stated explicitly and children need to use inference to make the link between the two. Pick out the different bits of magic that have taken place so far – the very fact that the tree produces a peach at all is a wonder, but then what happens?

Re-read the paragraph in Chapter 6 that begins: 'Something is about to happen...'. What causes James to feel this way?

Continue reading to the end of Chapter 10. Ask the children to look at the different and daring steps that James takes. At what points would a less brave (or desperate) child have turned back?

Reading Chapters 11 to 13, list the characters James encounters inside the peach. Use the illustrations as a checklist – and do not forget one final character introduced in Chapter 13. Ask the children to indicate which characters stand out as being most interesting – and to give reasons for their thinking, referring back to the text. Note the way in which the Centipede and the Silkworm are presented differently at this stage. One is very much in the foreground and the other taking up a role as a minor character.

Read to the end of Chapter 14 and ask the question: is James being kidnapped? Did anyone ask him if he wanted to go? Is this just how stories work or might the creatures have known this was the right thing for the boy?

Chapters 15 to 21

Read together from Chapter 15 to the end of Chapter 17. Ask the children to look at the two

Guided reading

different accounts of the peach making its way over Aunt Spiker and Aunt Sponge and out of the garden. This text provides an excellent opportunity to consider the varying points of view that can be taken in a story. Ask the children to think of their senses (sight, sound and so on) and review how the peach rolling is recounted in different ways from two points of view. What would the aunts have seen? What would the creatures have seen? Add in a third perspective – a bystander watching the whole event. What would they have seen?

Quickly ask the children if they can find a reference to another famous Dahl story in Chapter 16. (*Charlie and the Chocolate Factory*.)

Re-read the end of Chapter 16, from: 'Would it ever stop?' to the last line. How does Dahl build up the suspense? Ask the children to take their time quietly reading it aloud. Which parts keep the reader waiting to know what happens? Dahl pauses to tell us facts about the nature of round objects and the dangers of the cliffs. How do these add to the pace of the story?

Look at the scene inside the peach in Chapter 17. Pick out the different ways in which the characters have responded to this journey. Note the different reactions from the Old-Green-Grasshopper, Centipede and Earthworm.

Ask the children to read to the end of Chapter 19, where the issues of food – theirs and the sharks – are explored. Then ask the children to read to the end of Chapter 21. Using a large sheet of paper, ask them to draw a diagram, showing how the different components of James's grand plan fit together.

Chapters 22 to 28

Read together Chapters 22 and 23 where James's plan is put into action. Ask the children to look at the final page of Chapter 22 and to refer back to the final page of Chapter 16. What are the similarities between these two sections of the book? (There is a build up of suspense.) Can the children pick out common features (such as the similarity between the journey 'Down...down...' and the adding on of seagull after seagull)? How

do these contribute to the ways in which the suspense is built up?

As they begin reading Chapters 24 and 25, ask the children to each take responsibility for noting what they find out about one of the characters: Old-Green-Grasshopper, Earthworm, Ladybird, Spider and Centipede. What does each of these characters tell or show the reader about what they are like – both in the story and in real life?

Read Chapter 26 together. Can the children think of other stories with similar daring rescues? (*Spiderman*, *Batman* and so on.)

Continue to the end of Chapter 28. Look at the encounter with the Cloud-Men. At this point the character of the Centipede again comes to the fore. Ask the children to pick out the various ways in which he is central to this episode. (His rudeness, not staying quiet, ending up covered in paint.) In years to come, how would the Centipede recall this time? Would he be economical with the truth?

Chapters 29 to 33

Ask the children to read Chapters 29 and 30. Here the peach encounters the last problem before the end of the story. Focusing on Chapter 30, ask the children to give their opinion of the character of the Centipede. Why do readers love him? Why might they think he is annoying? Would it be more satisfying if he stayed covered in paint? Re-read the description of the water gushing in Chapter 30. Close the book and see how many of the wonderful verbs the children can remember.

Read Chapter 31 together. This is a beautiful moment in the story. Ask the children to think of words that describe the sorts of feeling this chapter evokes, then to find specific sentences in this chapter that add to that feeling. The bat-like creature is a mysterious presence in the story. Ask the children to read it and consider what feelings it evokes. Would we miss it if it wasn't in the story?

Let the children read up to the end of Chapter 33. Review together Chapter 33 and imagine some of the telephone calls that are being made.

What do the people think is floating above their city? What might they do in response to the threat of the peach?

Chapter 34 to the end

Read Chapter 34 and ask the children to predict ahead. If they know how the story ends, ask them to predict what the natural conclusion would be to such a turn of events. Do they think readers would expect a tragic ending to the story? If not, can the children explain why not? What various lucky escapes can they imagine?

Read on up to the end of Chapter 36. Check that the children are familiar with the Empire State Building – you could search the internet for a photograph.

In Chapter 37, James introduces the creatures to New York. Ask the children to split the poem up and practise a performance of the poem. Children could take a verse each and build their verses into a group performance.

Read to the end of the story and ask the children to compare the three different homes James has lived in – the aunts' house, the travelling peach and the peach stone in the park. How do the three differ from each other? Which part of the description in that final chapter do they find the most heart-warming and satisfying?

Shared reading

Extract 1

- Open a peach and look at a cross-section, then invite the children to imagine a tunnel through it. What would it be like?
- Read Extract 1 together and ask the children to imagine the experience of crawling through that peach. Encourage them to look for clues in the passage, and in their own imagining of the experience, to answer questions about how this would look, taste, smell and feel.
- Ask the children to point out the different risks James has taken by the time he reaches the door. What else could he have done? Tease out the fact that there is nothing for him to return to.
- Ask the children who knows the story and who doesn't. When James enters the stone and hears the voices, what might somebody new to the story think and feel? Is it a pleasant moment? Is it exciting? Scary?
- Why is that first scene in the peach stone so scary? What effect does the door vanishing create? Make sure the children are aware that, at that point, there is no turning back for James. He is trapped.

Extract 2

- Cover the last lines of the third, fourth and fifth stanzas, and the whole of the last stanza. Ask the children to pick out the words that provide the poem's rhyme structure, annotating links between rhyming words. Can the children make suggestions to complete the covered lines?
- Ask the children to look across the poem and consider what the stanzas have in common. What phrases and ideas are repeated? (For example, 'We may see...' and the different fantastic beasts.)
- Ask pairs to select a favourite stanza and practise reading it aloud. Let volunteers give their rendition. Try to build up a sucession of readers to perform the whole text.
- Read to the end of the sixth stanza. Explain the term 'Horns of a dilemma' (the two prongs of a difficult choice or situation).
- What is the mood of the poem? Is it sad, happy or scary? How does the centipede feel about the possiblity of encountering these creatures? Having read to the last stanza what sort of mood do they think they will uncover in the closing lines.
- Uncover the last stanza. How does this change the mood of the poem?

Extract 3

- Ask the children to give their impressions of the Centipede. Draw out the twin qualities of him being likeable as well as a bit of a pain.
- Read the opening of Chapter 26, and then look at the third extract together. How is falling off typical of the Centipede? (He is fun – but a pest.)
- Look at the extract as far as: '...flood of tears'. What is James planning to do? What are the dangers of such a plan?
- Ask volunteers to role-play the conversation. What is the difference between the Ladybird and the Earthworm?
- Consider the sentence that begins 'Suddenly'. What do the 'sharp tugs' signal? Is everything safe now?
- Read to the end of the passage. How is that over-the-top response to events so typical of the Centipede? In what ways have all the characters acted typically, for them?
- Split the class into small groups. Ask each group to look at different characters' responses to these events. What does this tell you about those characters?

Extract 1

He crawled in.

He kept on crawling.

This isn't a hole, he thought excitedly. *It's a tunnel!*

The tunnel was damp and murky, and all around him there was the curious bittersweet smell of fresh peach. The floor was soggy under his knees, the walls were wet and sticky, and peach juice was dripping from the ceiling. James opened his mouth and caught some of it on his tongue. It tasted delicious.

He was crawling uphill now, as though the tunnel were leading straight towards the very centre of the gigantic fruit. Every few seconds he paused and took a bite out of the wall. The peach flesh was sweet and juicy, and marvellously refreshing.

He crawled on for several more yards, and then suddenly – *bang* – the top of his head bumped into something extremely hard blocking his way. He glanced up. In front of him there was a solid wall that seemed at first as though it were made of wood. It certainly felt like wood, except that it was very jagged and full of deep grooves.

'Good heavens!' he said. 'I know what this is! I've come to the stone in the middle of the peach!'

Then he noticed that there was a small door cut into the face of the peach stone. He gave a push. It swung open. He crawled through it, and before he had time to glance up and see where he was, he heard a voice saying, '*Look* who's here!' And another one said, 'We've been *waiting* for you!'

James stopped and stared at the speakers, his face white with horror.

He started to stand up, but his knees were shaking so much he had to sit down again on the floor. He glanced behind him, thinking he could bolt back into the tunnel the way he had come, but the doorway had disappeared. There was now only a solid brown wall behind him.

Text © Roald Dahl

Extract 2

'We may see a Creature with forty-nine heads
Who lives in the desolate snow,
And whenever he catches a cold (which he dreads)
He has forty-nine noses to blow.

'We may see the venomous Pink-Spotted Scrunch
Who can chew up a man with one bite.
It likes to eat five of them roasted for lunch
And eighteen for its supper at night.

'We may see a Dragon, and nobody knows
That we won't see a Unicorn there.
We may see a terrible Monster with toes
Growing out of the tufts of his hair.

'We may see the sweet little Biddy-Bright Hen
So playful, so kind and well-bred;
And such beautiful eggs! You just boil them and then
They explode and they blow off your head.

'A Gnu and a Gnocerous surely you'll see
And that gnormous and gnorrible Gnat
Whose sting when it stings you goes in at the knee
And comes out through the top of your hat.

'We may even get lost and be frozen by frost.
We may die in an earthquake or tremor.
Or nastier still, we may even be tossed
On the horns of a furious Dilemma.

'But who cares! Let us go from this horrible hill!
Let us roll! Let us bowl! Let us plunge!
Let's go rolling and bowling and spinning until
We're away from old Spiker and Sponge!'

Text © Roald Dahl

Extract 3

'Silkworm!' yelled James. 'Quick! Start spinning!'

The Silkworm sighed, for she was still very tired from spinning all that silk for the seagulls, but she did as she was told.

'I'm going down after him!' cried James, grabbing the silk string as it started coming out of the Silkworm and tying the end of it around his waist. 'The rest of you hold on to Silkworm so I don't pull her over with me, and later on, if you feel three tugs on the string, start hauling me up again!'

He jumped, and he went tumbling down after the Centipede, down, down, down towards the sea below, and you can imagine how quickly the Silkworm had to spin to keep up with the speed of his fall.

'We'll never see either of them again!' cried the Ladybird. 'Oh, dear! Oh dear! Just when we were all so happy, too!'

Miss Spider, the Glow-worm, and the Ladybird all began to cry. So did the Earthworm. 'I don't care a bit about the Centipede,' the Earthworm sobbed. 'But I really did love that little boy.'

Very softly, the Old-Green-Grasshopper started to play the Funeral March on his violin, and by the time he had finished, everyone, including himself, was in a flood of tears.

Suddenly, there came three sharp tugs on the rope. 'Pull!' shouted the Old-Green-Grasshopper. 'Everyone get behind me and pull!'

There was about a mile of string to be hauled in, but they all worked like mad, and in the end, over the side of the peach, there appeared a dripping-wet James with a dripping-wet Centipede clinging to him tightly with all forty-two of his legs.

'He saved me!' gasped the Centipede.

Text © Roald Dahl

Plot, character and setting

Boundaries

> **Objective:** To identify and understand the theme of a story.
> **What you need:** Skipping ropes, large space (for example, the hall), pens and pieces of blank card.

What to do

● Point out that, in the book, a number of rules are broken – those created by adults like the aunts, and also the *laws of nature*. (For example: peaches do not fly!)

● Organise the children to work with a partner, with a skipping rope placed between them. Explain that the rope represents *a boundary*: one side represents 'normal', where the rules are kept and the other side 'magical', where the rules are broken.

● Let the partners decide which side they are each going to stand on. Hand out pens and card.

● Invite the children to write pairs of labels: one partner writing the 'normal' and the other the 'broken rule' from the story. So if a child writes 'A giant peach' for the magical side, their partner should write 'Small peaches' for the normal side.

● Ask the children to compare their results with other pairs to see if they have found all of the magical occurrences.

● Finally, ask if the children can remember where, in the story, rules are broken. (After the old man appears, James's actions when his aunts send him out at night, the giant creatures, the peach's escape, the shark attack.) Ask the children to make a note of these places.

> **Differentiation**
> **For older/more able children:** Ask the children to create a third set of labels, listing the rules that are broken by these different events in the story.
> **For younger/less able children:** Encourage the children to think of some of the magical events in the story. What difference does the magic make?

Misery

> **Objective:** To explore the ways events influence characters.
> **What you need:** Copies of *James and the Giant Peach*, long strips of paper, pens of three different colours.
> **Cross-curricular links:** PSHE.

What to do

● Ask the children to consider the events that take place in the opening chapters of the story. Encourage the children to itemise the different miseries that James experiences.

● Challenge the children to write the most miserable list they can think of on the strips of paper, using a colour code as follows:

  ● one colour for miseries *read* in the story (for example: What happens to James when the other children come to see the peach?).

  ● another colour for *imagined* miseries, extending beyond the story itself (for example, the reader might imagine that James's room is cold, though it is not actually written in the text).

● Once they have created a very long list, tell the children to take the third pen and decide on three miseries that they think are the most awful and circle these.

● Ask the children to write short quotes from James expressing how he feels faced with these miseries.

> **Differentiation**
> **For older/more able children:** Ask the children to write a paragraph about one of the imagined miseries. For example, they could write a scene in which James asks if he can have some wood for the fireplace in his room.
> **For younger/less able children:** Give the children a list of points in the story and ask them the question: 'What is sad at this point?'

Plot, character and setting

Setting diagrams

> **Objective:** To understand how settings influence events and incidents in stories.
> **What you need:** Copies of *James and the Giant Peach*, large sheets of paper, drawing materials.
> **Cross-curricular links:** Art and design; ICT.

What to do
● Use this activity after reading as far as Chapter 26.
● Invite the children to think about the settings of the house on the hill and the peach.
● Ask the children to list some of the features of the two settings. (For example: James's room in the house and the surrounding countryside; the tunnel in the peach, and so on.) One way of doing this is to imagine walking (or crawling) into the settings. What would they see and feel?
● Organise the children to work in groups of four. Hand out paper and drawing materials. Say

that you want each group to create diagrams of these two settings. Two of the children should work on the diagram of the peach and the other two on the house.
● Explain that the diagram should contain a picture of the location and arrows pointing out specific places within it, as well as mentioning events that took place in these various locations. The diagram of the peach could include a reference to the side where the Centipede fell and the one of the house might show the fence around the peach.

> **Differentiation**
> **For older/more able children:** Ask the children to include labels showing how James felt during any events that took place in the setting.
> **For younger/less able children:** Let the children draw their diagram and add picture labels, rather than writing.

Point of view

> **Objective:** To change point of view, for example, retell incidents from the point of view of another character.
> **What you need:** Copies of *James and the Giant Peach*, whiteboards and pens, tape recorder, props and dressing-up clothes (optional).
> **Cross-curricular links:** Drama.

What to do
● Use this activity after reading the first 15 chapters of the story.
● Invite the children to imagine that they are either Aunt Sponge or Aunt Spiker and to imagine events from their point of view. Remember that these characters are villians. Encourage them to re-read some conversations to remind them how these villians talk.
● Ask the children, in pairs, to write a scripted dialogue between the aunts at any stage in the story. For example, the children could write

the words the two aunts said to each other the night they sent James out to clear up, or even the conversation they had after they had peeled themselves off the grass following their flattening. (We are not actually told that the peach killed them!) They can use Roald Dahl's words, as a starter, but should then create their own lines.
● Give the children time to rehearse their dialogue. Then let pairs perform their piece in front of the rest of the class, perhaps using props and dressing-up clothes. Record some of the examples on your tape recorder.

> **Differentiation**
> **For older/more able children:** Ask the children to write up their scripted dialogue as a newspaper interview.
> **For younger/less able children:** Let the children draw pictures, using speech bubbles to record what the aunts say to each other.

Plot, character and setting

Danger!

> **Objective:** To identify dilemmas faced by characters and discuss how characters deal with them.
> **What you need:** Photocopiable page 15, cut up into 'Danger' and 'Saved' cards.

What to do
● Organise the children in to groups of two and three.
● Ask the children to think of the dangers they remember from stories they have read or seen. Encourage examples from their favourite films and television shows, as well as traditional tales and favourite books.
● Hand out the 'Danger' cards, but do not provide the children with the 'Saved' cards yet. Tell the children to read through the different dangers encountered in *James and the Giant Peach*.

● Ask the children if they can recall the way in which the characters were saved from each of these dangers.
● Now hand out the 'Saved' cards and ask the children to place both these and the 'Danger' cards face down and shuffled.
● Challenge the children to take turns picking up two cards, the aim being to select a 'Danger' and 'Saved' that match. When the children make a match, they collect the two cards and score a point. The winner is the one with the most points. If the cards do not match, the children must replace them face down.

> **Differentiation**
> **For older/more able children:** Ask the children to write their own 'Saved' cards, based on the story.
> **For younger/less able children:** Ask the children to read and match the cards before playing the game.

Character detectives

> **Objective:** To identify the main characteristics of key characters.
> **What you need:** Copies of *James and the Giant Peach*, photocopiable page 16, pencils, pens.

What to do
● Ask the children to work in pairs and give each couple a copy of the photocopiable sheet.
● Let the children read through the character traits in the first column of the sheet, checking that they understand them. Explain that a trait is a quality or characteristic displayed by a character.
● Looking at the list at the bottom of the page, ask the children to match each of the characters to one of the traits.
● Suggest, as a first step, the children pencil in their guesses without referring to the book. They can compare their results with others and see if their guesses differ.
● Then ask the children to look at the book

finding and noting a page that justifies that match. If, for example, they decide the Earthworm matches the trait 'Very juicy', they need to find a page that justifies this. (Chapter 20: '…the biggest, fattest, pinkest, juiciest Earthworm in the world.')
● Encourage the children to skim through the book and find sentences to quote. If they are struggling, you can direct them to Chapters 2, 3, 14, 20, 24, 26 and 27.
● Ask the children to compare their answers with another pair. Have they matched the same characters and traits?

> **Differentiation**
> **For older/more able children:** Varying levels of support can be given to children hunting for quotes, according to their ability to skim read the text.
> **For younger/less able children:** Instead of finding quotes, let the children write a short sentence to support their reasoning, for example: 'Worms are juicy.'

Plot, character and setting

Lift off

> **Objective:** To retell the main points of a story in sequence.
> **What you need:** Copies of *James and the Giant Peach*, photocopiable page 17, scissors, glue sticks, paper.

What to do
● Plan this activity over two days. On the first day, ask the children to re-read the sequence of events from Chapter 19, where the peach is being eaten, to the end of Chapter 22, where the characters are flying safely away.
● Encourage the children to make connections between one event leading to another in the text – but do not actually make a list with them. For example, the use of the Earthworm as bait results in seagulls being attached to the peach.
● On the second day, ask the children to work without copies of the book. Can they recall the basic outline of events in the story that they covered in the previous session?
● Organise the children into pairs, giving each couple the photocopiable sheet, paper, scissors and glue.
● Invite the children to cut out the cards and place them in the correct sequential order. They should then stick them onto the paper.
● Encourage the children to talk in their pairs, making the connection of one event leading to or caused by another. Stress that this is a really vital insight into a story.

> **Differentiation**
> **For older/more able children:** Ask the children to annotate their completed sequence with notes showing the connections between events.
> **For younger/less able children:** Make notes on the first day and let the children refer back to these.

Quentin Blake's storytelling

> **Objective:** To take account of viewpoint, explaining how events may look from a different point of view.
> **What you need:** Photocopiable page 18, scissors, A3 paper, pencils.

What to do
● Ask the children what effect they think the pictures have on the story of *James and the Giant Peach*.
● Hand out copies of the photocopiable sheet, scissors and paper and ask the children to work individually.
● Tell the children to cut out the pictures and place them in the correct sequential order. They can first go through each recalling what event it illustrates. Can the children recall when each event shown in the illustration took place – and what was happening?
● Ask the children to focus on the characters in the pictures. What would they have been thinking at these points in the story?
● Let the children stick the pictures onto their sheet of A3 paper, leaving room around each of the images for writing.
● Invite the children to work through the pictures and to create thought bubbles for each of the characters.
● Point out that, in one scene, different characters may be thinking different things – so the illustration with the Centipede and Earthworm will involve very different views on the idea of the Earthworm acting as seagull bait.
● Share some of the children's ideas.

> **Differentiation**
> **For older/more able children:** Ask the children to draw two extra scenes that are not shown in the story – such as James pleading with his aunts to be allowed to join the peach crowds. These can be annotated in the same way.
> **For younger/less able children:** Let the children select four of the pictures and say what they think a particular character may be thinking.

Danger!

Danger James is sent out on his own in the cold and lonely night.	**Danger** The peach falls off a cliff.
Saved He finds a tunnel leading into the peach stone.	**Saved** It lands in the sea.
Danger James drops and loses all the magic things he was given by the old man.	**Saved** James points out that they can eat some peach.
Saved The magic things get to work on the peach tree and the creatures in the earth.	**Danger** The peach is attacked by sharks.
Danger The peach is attached to the tree in the garden of the cruel aunts.	**Saved** James attaches seagulls to the peach and it flies.
Saved The Centipede nibbles through the stem.	**Danger** The Cloud-Men throw hailstones at the peach.
Danger The Earthworm says that there is no food and they are going to starve.	**Saved** James and the creatures escape back into the peach.

Plot, character and setting

Character detectives

Trait	Character
Brave and kind	
Very short, with piggy eyes	
Tall, lean and bony	
Loud and cheerful	
Very juicy	
Mysterious and magical	
Old, gentle and musical	
Huge and wispy	

Aunt Spiker   The Centipede   The Earthworm

The old man   James

The Old-Green-Grasshopper   The Cloud-Men   Aunt Sponge

Lift off

Everyone persuades the Earthworm to be bait.
James explains his plan.
James loops seagull number five hundred and one.
James pulls the Earthworm away from the first seagull.
James shouts, 'Here we go!'.
One shark signals to the other shark.
The Centipede cries, 'Look!'.
The first seagull flies through the loop of silk.
The first seagull starts swooping down.
The first shark lunges at the peach.
The five-hundred-and-second seagull is caught.
The peach rises out of the water.
The Spider and Silkworm start spinning.

Quentin Blake's storytelling

Illustrations © Quentin Blake

 SCHOLASTIC
www.scholastic.co.uk

READ & RESPOND: Activities based on James and the Giant Peach

Talk about it

Best moment

> **Objective:** To express their views about a story.
> **What you need:** Blank cards, pens, paper clips.

What to do

● Organise the children to work in groups of three or four, handing a pile of small cards to each team.

● Ask each child to think through their reading of *James and the Giant Peach* and make a note of the best moments from the story on the cards. Encourage each child to think of four or five incidents and then to share their ideas with the rest of the group.

● Some children will have suggested the same moments and these cards should be clipped together. Ask the groups to aim for between ten and 20 separate incidents in total.

● Once they have their set of cards, ask the children to try and agree a ranked order for these cards, with the best incident at the top and others in order below.

● Point out that they will need to discuss reasons for ranking particular events high or low on the list, carefully explaining their choices. Also, remind the children to let every member of the group have a say, using good listening skills.

● Share some of the groups' ideas as a class.

> **Differentiation**
> **For older/more able children:** Ask the children to write a paragraph giving an overview of the results from all the groups. For example, is there an event that is commonly ranked highly?
> **For younger/less able children:** Let the children list their favourite events in the story and explain their choices to the rest of their group.

Times and feelings

> **Objective:** To discuss characters' feelings, referring to the text.
> **What you need:** Copies of *James and the Giant Peach*, photocopiable page 22, different colour pens.
> **Cross-curricular links:** PSHE.

What to do

● Use this activity after reading at least halfway through the story.

● Organise the children to work in pairs, providing each pair with photocopiable page 22 and pens.

● Encourage the children to list as many different feelings they think the characters in the story could have experienced in the first column on the sheet. They could range from the immediate examples ('happy') to the more obscure ones ('jealous', 'desolate'). Encourage the pairs to discuss their ideas, writing their notes in the 'Feelings' column.

● Then, ask the children to make a brief list in the right-hand column of events that took place in the story. They can skim through the book for ideas but must write in their own words.

● Using a different colour pen, ask the children to draw lines connecting feelings to events – so they may link 'happy' with James being safe in the peach. The children should add to the chart as they work to make sure each event has a connected emotion.

● Encourage the children to write comments along the connecting lines – for example, if a feeling is being shown by a particular character.

● Ask the children to talk to another pair about the feelings they chose and the events which they linked them to.

> **Differentiation**
> **For older/more able children:** Let the children use a thesaurus to find new words for different feelings.
> **For younger/less able children:** Ask the children to list some of the events James experiences and, alongside, make a note of how he felt.

Talk about it

Cloud-Men

> **Objective:** To identify the main characteristics of characters, drawing on the text to justify views.
> **What you need:** Copies of *James and the Giant Peach*, cotton wool and small circular stickers (optional).
> **Cross-curricular links:** Art and design; Drama.

What to do
● Ask the children to look carefully at the section of the book where the peach encounters the Cloud-Men (Chapters 27 to 32).
● Organise the children to work in groups of two or three. Ask the children to spend a bit of time discussing these two questions:
 ● What were the Cloud-Men like?
 ● How do we know what they were like?
● Encourage the children to form an opinion and find parts of the story that support their opinions. They can make brief notes to record these.
● Ask the children to think of other storylines that could take place with the Cloud-Men, either as a variation on the book (for example, the Cloud-Men being helpful characters) or as an extension (for example, an incident where James helps the Cloud-Men and forms a friendship with them).
● As an optional addition to the activity, let the children make their own Cloud-Men from loosely rolled cotton-wool shapes with circular stickers as eyes. These could be used to role-play a retelling of their new story. Some children could demonstrate their storyline, using these models, for the class.

> **Differentiation**
> **For older/more able children:** Ask the children to devise a new story about the Cloud-Men.
> **For younger/less able children:** Encourage the children to use their cotton-wool Cloud-Men to role-play any scene from the story or imaginative encounter.

Character voices

> **Objective:** To identify main characteristics of characters.
> **What you need:** Paper and pens, tape recorder (optional).

What to do
● Arrange the children into groups of three and four. Ask the children to make a shared list of the most memorable characters from the story – perhaps two each.
● In their groups, tell the children to think of different incidents in which each of these characters is involved.
● Ask them to think of the sorts of things these characters would say at those times – for example, what sort of thing would Aunt Spiker say as the peach starts to roll towards her? Stress that the children do not need to remember or quote the text – they need to think of the sort of thing a character might say, based on known characteristics.
● Add the condition that the children must try saying their lines in the style of the character concerned, so they must adopt an appropriate voice and manner.
● Hand out the paper and pens and invite the children to work individually, writing down some of the quotes they have devised.
● Allow time for sharing and performing quotes.

> **Differentiation**
> **For older/more able children:** Record some of the performances to create 'a cinema trailer', in which characters are briefly encountered giving quick one-liners.
> **For younger/less able children:** Ask the children to create just one or two quotes for the characters and share them with the group.

Talk about it

Cut-out characters

> **Objective:** To retell scenes from the story.
> **What you need:** Copies of *James and the Giant Peach*, photocopiable page 23 copied onto card, scissors, drawing materials.
> **Cross-curricular links:** Art and design; Drama.

What to do
- Hand out photocopiable page 23. Ask the children to follow the instructions on the sheet to cut out and build the characters. Children may want to colour them in.
- Organise the children to work in pairs, re-creating and role-playing a scene from *James and the Giant Peach*.
- Encourage the children to include the conversations that take place between characters, referring to the book if necessary. You could ask them to find some of the longest conversations in the book.
- Invite the children to use the characters to create scenes that do not take place in the story – for example they could role-play an encounter between the Centipede and aunts. What would they say to each other?
- Ask the children to agree on one good idea for an additional scene. Encourage them to discuss and develop their thoughts as to what the characters might say. Stress that the children should work together closely, making suggestions and listening to their partner.
- Groups can perform their scene to the class.

> **Differentiation**
> **For older/more able children:** Using their additional scene idea, ask the children to write a short playscript developing the dialogue.
> **For younger/less able children:** You may need to cut out the characters for the children. Ask them to focus on re-creating scenes from the book.

Other stories

> **Objective:** To retell the main points of a story.
> **What you need:** Photocopiable page 24, felt-tipped pens, A3 paper, scissors, glue.

What to do
- Organise the children to work in small groups. Hand out the photocopiable sheet and explain that each box refers to a story feature.
- Select the feature 'A child is sent to live with horrible relatives'. Does this remind the children of anything in *James and the Giant Peach?* (James living with Aunt Sponge and Spiker.) Can they retell this part of the story?
- Tell the groups to go through the sheet in the same way, orally retelling the related episodes from *James and the Giant Peach*.
- Ask the children if the features on the sheet remind them of any other stories. Let them discuss ideas in their groups. (Suggestions for 'There is a magical, flying journey' might include *The Snowman* or *Chitty Chitty Bang Bang*.)
- Ask each group to agree on the feature they think will provide the greatest list of other stories. Let the children cut out their chosen feature and stick it at the centre of a large piece of paper. They now need to write the names of their other stories around the page.
- Encourage different groups to help each other. This could be a class challenge to create the most extensive set of lists. A different feature could be placed on different tables and the groups could have an allocated time at each table. Which feature is found in the greatest number of titles?

> **Differentiation**
> **For older/more able children:** Ask groups to make up a story combining two of the features.
> **For younger/less able children:** Let the group select from just four features and think of one or two other stories.

Talk about it

Times and feelings

Fill in this table with examples from the story. The first three 'feelings' have been provided for you. Then draw lines to match feelings to events.

Feelings	Events
Happy	
Jealous	
Desolate	

SECTION
5

Cut-out characters

Cut around each character. Fold the tabs back to make them stand up.

Illustrations © Quentin Blake

Talk about it

Other stories

Look at the story features in the boxes below. Can you remember examples of these features in *James and the Giant Peach*?

How many other stories can you think of that contain any of these features?

A child is sent to live with horrible relatives.	There is a magical, flying journey.
There are animals that can talk.	Someone goes down a tunnel.
Someone is given some special things that can do magic.	The characters are attacked by frightening creatures.
A miserable child escapes to a happy, new life.	Two of the characters are always arguing.

Get writing

Character memories

> **Objective:** To take account of the viewpoint of a narrator.
> **What you need:** Sheets of writing paper, pens, one large sheet of paper, computers (optional), badges: 'Interviewer', 'Listener', 'Character' (optional).
> **Cross-curricular links:** ICT.

What to do

- Arrange the children into groups of three, each child in the group being either 'A', 'B' or 'C'.
- Explain that they each need to pick a different character from the story. If two are vying for the same one (and it is usually the Centipede), then this can be decided by a toss of a coin.
- Tell the children there are three ways of taking part – as a character, an interviewer who asks them questions, or a listener who chips in and helps the conversation along. The interviewer and listener are to find out as much as they can about the character. They can wear one of the badges to idicate their role.
- Start with child 'A' being the character, child 'B' interviewing and child 'C' being the listener. Allow five minutes for the interview. As the character is talking, *both* the interviewer and listener should take notes.
- Swap roles over, so that each child takes a turn in each role.
- Explain that, in newspaper reporting, several participants in an event can be interviewed. Ask the children to write up a shared news report, using their notes. The final news reports could be transferred onto computer.

> **Differentiation**
> **For older/more able children:** Ask groups to script a short television programme based on their interviews.
> **For younger/less able children:** Let one child be their character and the other two both be interviewers.

Create dangers

> **Objective:** To plot a sequence of episodes modelled on a known story.
> **What you need:** Long strips of paper, small paper rectangles, pens, glue.

What to do

- Ask the children to work in pairs, beginning by retelling the events of the central sequence in the book, where the peach is first attacked by sharks, then flies, then is attacked by the Cloud-Men.
- Point out the way this sequence depends on dangers occurring followed by escapes. Such sequences are made up of smaller dangers sewn together. (For example: the Cloud-Men incident includes the paint problem.)
- Using the small rectangles of paper, ask the children to construct a set of dangers through which a character of their creation could pass. They need to agree on a name for their character and some of his or her traits. Each danger should be written on a separate piece of paper, followed by the escape.
- Once the children have created their series of linked dangers, ask them if they can squeeze any further rectangles between those they have already created.
- Then ask the children to think of a suitable start and end for this story.
- Finally let the children stick their rectangles in order onto the paper strip, creating their storyboard for a dangerous adventure.
- Ask the children to share their storyboards with the rest of the class.

> **Differentiation**
> **For older/more able children:** Ask the children to write up a scene from the adventure, including the character's thoughts.
> **For younger/less able children:** Reduce the number of incidents required.

Get writing

Way in to magic

> **Objective:** To plan a story, identifying the stages of its telling.
> **What you need:** Paper and pens, various objects, for example: key, clothes peg, spoon, walking stick.

What to do
● Re-read Chapter 3 together. Prompt the children towards thinking about the old man and how he transforms James's life by giving him the magical things. Talk through the events that follow. Note what James was meant to do, what actually happened and the later explanation from the creatures concerning the magical things.
● Invite the children to look at your collection of objects and to think of the ways in which these could be used in a story to transform someone's life.
● Let each child choose an object and a character, of their creation, who could be given it, and then to plan the 'before' and 'after' for their

character's encounter with it. These are crucial stages in magical stories (look at 'Cinderella', for instance).
● Ask the children to fold a piece of paper in half and to make notes about what life was like before the magic on one half, and after on the other.
● Next, tell the children to decide how the magic object makes its way into the life of their character to transform his or her life. Let them write this part of the story.
● Encourage the children to complete their narrative in stages, using more than one writing session, if necessary.

> **Differentiation**
> **For older/more able children:** Say that the magic item can be used more than once, to enable the children to extend their narrative.
> **For younger/less able children:** Ask the children to make notes for their narrative, focusing on one element of their story.

Character profiles

> **Objective:** To write portraits of characters.
> **What you need:** Photocopiable page 28, pens, drawing materials and computers (optional).
> **Cross-curricular links:** ICT, Art and Design.

What to do
● Talk through the ways in which characters are presented in stories, following the three headings on the photocopiable sheet. Ask the children if they can think of examples from the book to show how characters are portrayed through their appearance, actions and speech. Explain that 'speech' does not just need to include verbatim quotes. It can also include the types of things a character said or the manner in which they spoke.
● Hand out the photocopiable sheet and ask the children to look at the character profiles from *James and the Giant Peach*. Point out that there

is a mix of character roles: a hero, a helper and a villain.
● Ask the children to fill in the photocopiable sheet, devising three characters of their own and thinking about how their speech, actions and appearance could be used to show their personality. Ask them to try to be as original as possible in their ideas.
● Challenge the children to write up their character portraits from their notes. Let the children use computers to complete their work, if appropriate. Children could also draw pictures of their characters.

> **Differentiation**
> **For older/more able children:** Ask the children to use these characters to write a magical story scene.
> **For younger/less able children:** Limit the activity to two characters, focusing on creating a good character and a villain.

Get writing

Story map

Objective: To develop the use of settings in writing.
What you need: Photocopiable page 29, globe or atlas for each group, glue, pens and paper.
Cross-curricular links: Geography.

What to do
● Organise the children into groups of three, giving each group a copy of the photocopiable sheet, pens and paper, and a globe or atlas.
● Ask the groups to draw outlines of the places covered by the story (Great Britain and North America) on a large sheet of paper, using the atlas or globe as a guide.
● Tell them to cut out the white boxes and stick them on the map, adding arrows if needed.
● Ask them to make notes on the map indicating how each setting along the way contributes to the storyline. What particular problem or danger did each setting present to the characters?

● Next ask the children to cut out and place the shaded boxes – places not mentioned in the original text, where the peach could have encountered other adventures. They should make notes indicating adventures for these diversions.
● In their groups, ask the children to write notes for three new chapters for the story, based on ideas they have created on their story map.

Differentiation
For older/more able children: Using the same map, ask the children to create an original story in which another magical journey is taken along the same route. Make the rule that it cannot include a magical fruit!
For younger/less able children: Using the map, ask the children to write words and phrases or draw small symbols that show the various events that happened in the story and ask them to focus on completing notes for only one of the shaded boxes.

James prompts

Objective: To use different ways of planning stories.
What you need: Photocopiable page 30, scissors, paper and pens.

What to do
● Give the children each a copy of the photocopiable sheet and ask them to cut out the cards and place them face down on the table in a random order.
● Explain that these cards provide ideas from *James and the Giant Peach*, but will also point the children in the direction of their own story plan. Explain that they wont be copying the story but using ideas from it to stimulate their own creative writing, this is a common feature in writing.
● Let the children turn the cards face upwards one by one and think of how they can apply the idea displayed to a story of their own. Ask them to make notes.
● If they turn up a card and are completely

baffled, they can return it to the pile, but encourage them to do this only once.
● When they have planned out their story, ask the children to decide if any of the cards prompts an alternative idea. Can they think of another suggestion that would work better in the story? Sometimes the initial idea for a story needs changing once the fuller tale has been worked out.
● Once they are satisfied with their story plan, ask the children to try writing some selected scenes from it.
● Ask the children to share their ideas.

Differentiation
For older/more able children: Ask the children to develop their story idea over time and write out a fuller narrative.
For younger/less able children: Keep the cards face up and ask the children to select three in order to plan their story.

Character profiles

James	The Earthworm	Aunt Spiker
brave, kind, boy	long, pink, juicy	lean, tall, bony
rescues the Centipede when he falls of the peach	scared, doesn't want to be used as seagull bait	selfish, lazy and cruel
'I'm going down after him.'	'Oh I shall be pecked to death.'	screeching voice, shouting

Make notes below to create three character profiles of your own.

Hero	Helper	Villain

Story map

A school of whales	The Loch Ness monster

The rainbow	London Zoo

Land of the Cloud-Men	The white cliffs of Dover

The Arctic	London Eye

A school of sharks	The Queen Mary

New York	Aunts' house

Undersea kingdom	Grand Canyon

James prompts

A really good character.	Characters that are magically changed.
A cruel villain or pair of villains.	A problem that needs to be solved.
A gift that creates magic.	A team of characters who are very different.
A hazardous journey.	A scary part of a journey.
A danger from which to escape.	Angry and scary mysterious characters.

Assessment

Assessment advice

James and the Giant Peach provides a relatively simple storyline, heavily dominated by a small number of significant situations broken into smaller events. This makes it an ideal text on which to base assessment of the children's grasp of both storyline and character.

Find the end of any chapter in the book (except the last one) and ask the children about the way it concludes, focusing on the question: 'Why does it make us want to read the next chapter?'. Discuss how the author creates and builds up suspense throughout the story.

Beginning with the process of living with and escaping from the wicked aunts, establish the children's ability to pick out the order in which events take place. Can the children remember the story well – or are there events that they have forgotten? Building on this sequential order, use the central event of the shark attack and James's escape to establish the children's understanding of why certain events had to take place. If appropriate, use the cards on photocopiable page 32 to support the children's reasoning.

The story has a strong degree of overt characterisation. Roald Dahl tended to be very clear-cut about his characters. Talking through some of the main figures in the story, you can establish that the children have formed a view of them, and on what they are basing this view. They may have decided that the Centipede is a cheerful character. Elicit from the children how they have come to this conclusion. Can they point to incidents in the story to back up their thinking? What actions and words indicate the type of character James is? Do the children have a favourite character? Can they explain why?

Why?

> **Objective:** To explore the plot in a longer narrative.
> **What you need:** Copies of *James and the Giant Peach*, photocopiable page 32, scissors, paper, glue and pens.

What to do

● Ask the children to cut out the cards on the photocopiable sheet and place them in the order they think the questions should be answered. Explain to the children that they should work individually on this, and that there is no right or wrong order in which to position the cards – it is entirely their own choice.

● The children may come up with an ordering based on how important the questions are, or which ones are harder than others. Many will resort to the natural progression of events through the book.

● Once they have sequenced their cards, ask the children to read through the questions and to think of answers. Encourage them to make short notes at the bottom of each card, showing some of the key points they would make in their answer.

● Each of the questions is open to a range of answers not just a simple response. Encourage the children to think of more than one answer for each. For example: can they think of more than one feeling that could have been running through the Cloud-Men's minds?

● Having considered each card, ask the children to pick the two where they think they could give the best answer. Ask the children to stick these onto a sheet of writing paper and to write carefully their full answers underneath.

Why?

Why is James so unhappy?	Why does the peach grow?
Why are the creatures so big?	Why does the man give the magic things to James?
Why does the peach fly?	Why do the Cloud-Men attack?
Why does the peach float across the sea?	Why is the Centipede covered in paint?